Color Fairies
A Decorative Fantasy Coloring Book for Adults

Stephen John Smith

Copyright © 2017 Stephen John Smith

All rights reserved.

No part of this book may be reproduced, transmitted, or stored in any form or by any means except for your own personal use or for a book review, without the express written permission of the author:

artist@stephenjohnsmith.com

ISBN-13: 978-1544279497

ISBN-10: 1544279493

StephenJohnSmith.com

About this Book

I love fairies, flora, patterns, and all things magical, and I'm guessing you do too. As this book was a joy to create, I'm hoping you have as much fun coloring the images as I did drawing them.

A Suggestion

Rather than working directly on the pages of this book, you might consider working on copies. The advantages to this approach follow, but first, please read the Copyright sidebar.

Advantages of Working on Copies

- Using this method you won't need to worry about making mistakes. If you mess up, just make another photocopy and start again.
- Photocopying will allow you to use your favorite paper. Art suppliers provide literally hundreds of delicious choices.
- Working on copies gives you the freedom to experiment with many different color combinations and media for each image.

Paper Quality

As this book is constructed on medium weight paper, if you do decide to work on it directly you'll find that colored pencils, pastels, and crayons will give you the best results.

Remember to slide a stout backing sheet under the image you're working on to prevent your enthusiastic coloring strokes leaving dents in the pages beneath.

The paper in this book, as well as standard printer paper, will wrinkle and bleed through if you use wet media such as markers or watercolors. If you plan on using wet media, try photocopying to card stock, watercolor paper, or artist's specialty papers.

Copyright

As Copyright Law can be more than a little confusing, here is a quick summary of the purchaser's permissions and restrictions:

You MAY:

- Copy uncolored pages for your sole personal use.
- Post your finished/colored work online to share with others (e.g. in Facebook groups or in Amazon reviews, etc.).
- Give away your colored original pieces to anyone you wish.

You MAY NOT:

- Distribute copyrighted work, even if you paid for it.
- Post blank uncolored pages online.
- Give copies or scans of uncolored pages to someone else - even if it's a freebie posted by the artist.

The Art of Coloring

Coloring is such a personal creative adventure that there is no right or wrong way to go about it. Experimentation, and all its inevitable surprises, encourages one to learn and grow.

There is, however, one trick to coloring that seems to work every time -- relax, let your pen, pencil, marker, or brush lead you, and readily embrace all the joy that will surely come as you sink deeper and deeper into the coloring experience.

Simply put, coloring is a hoot! Have fun and watch your tensions melt away.

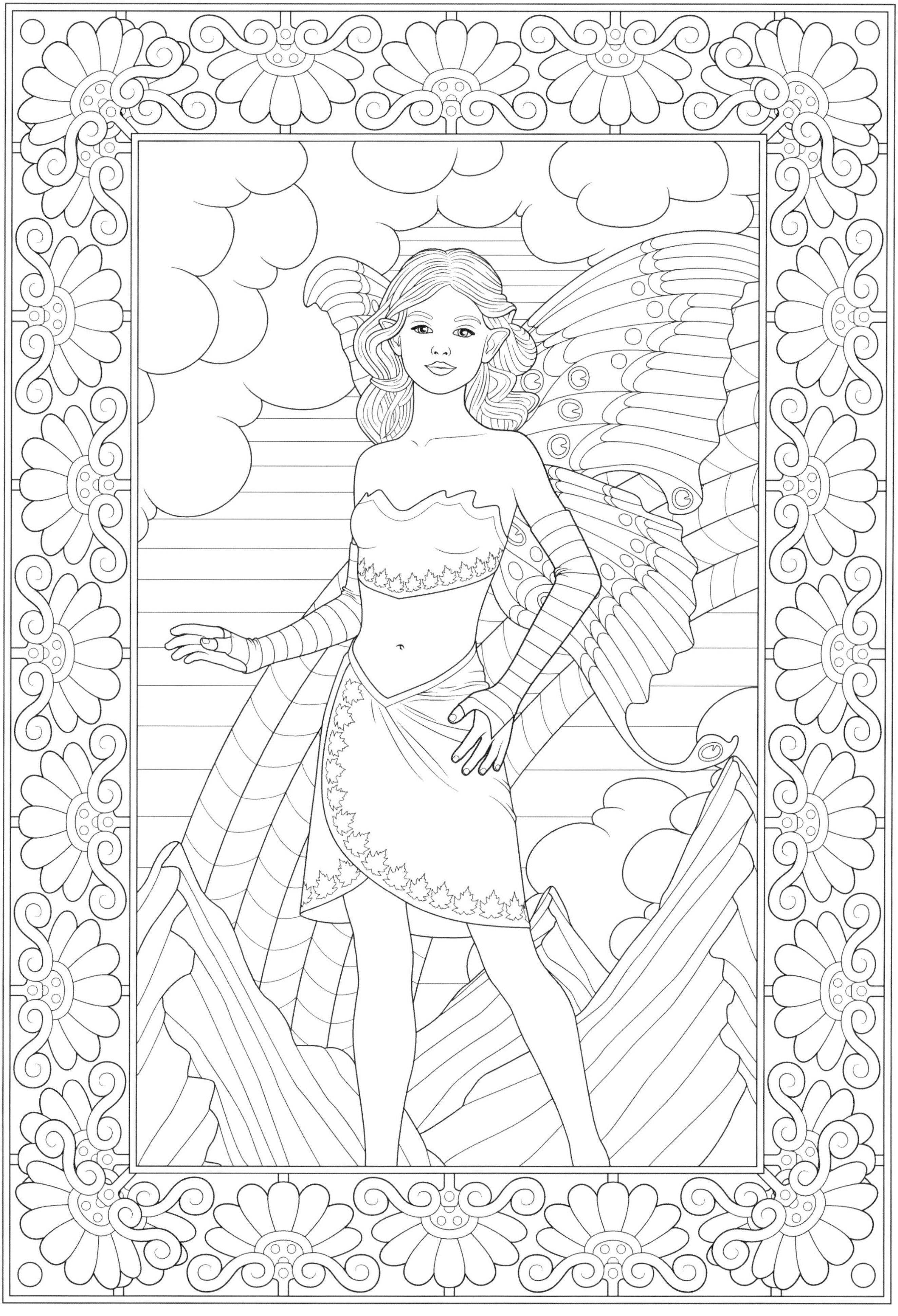

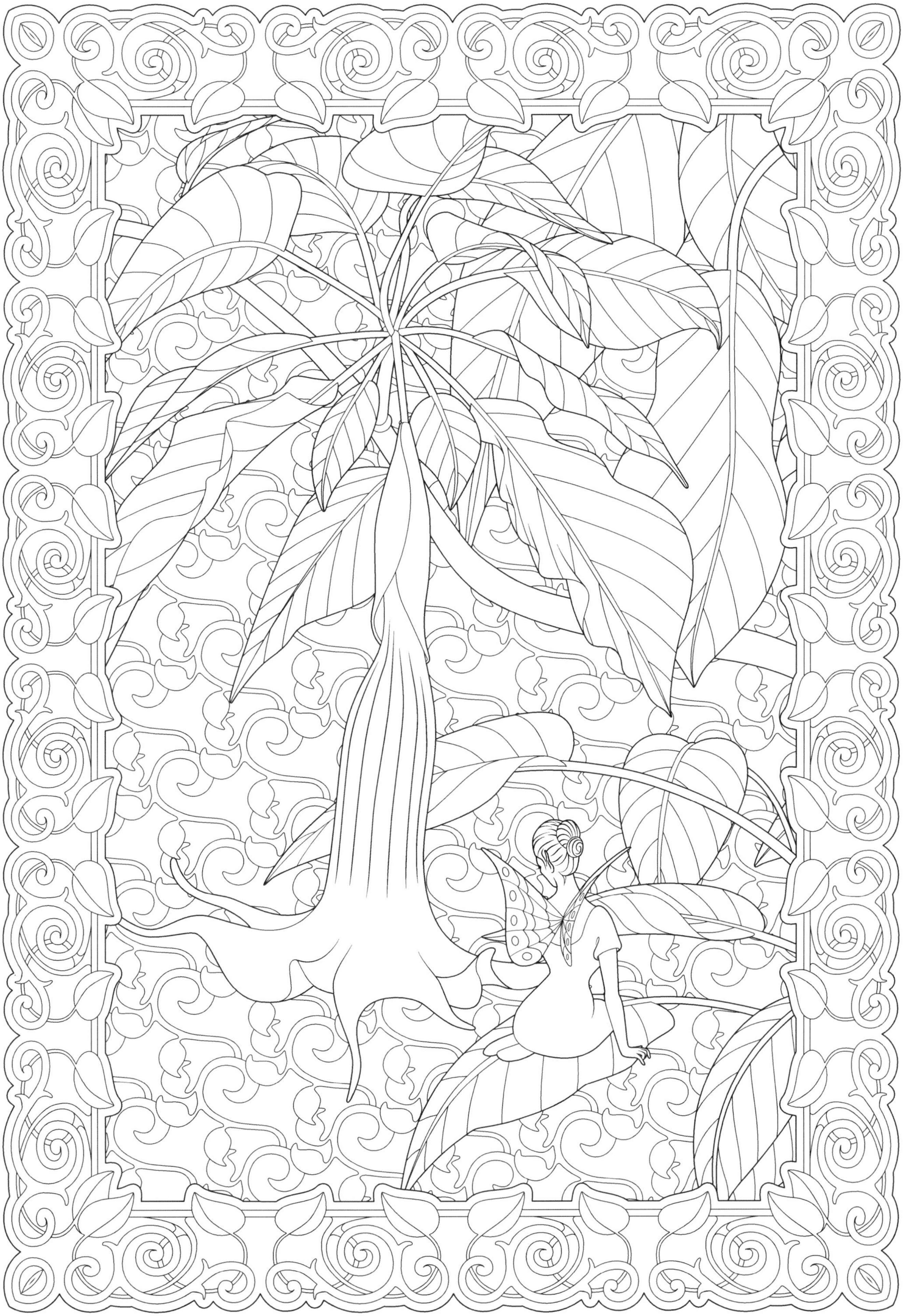

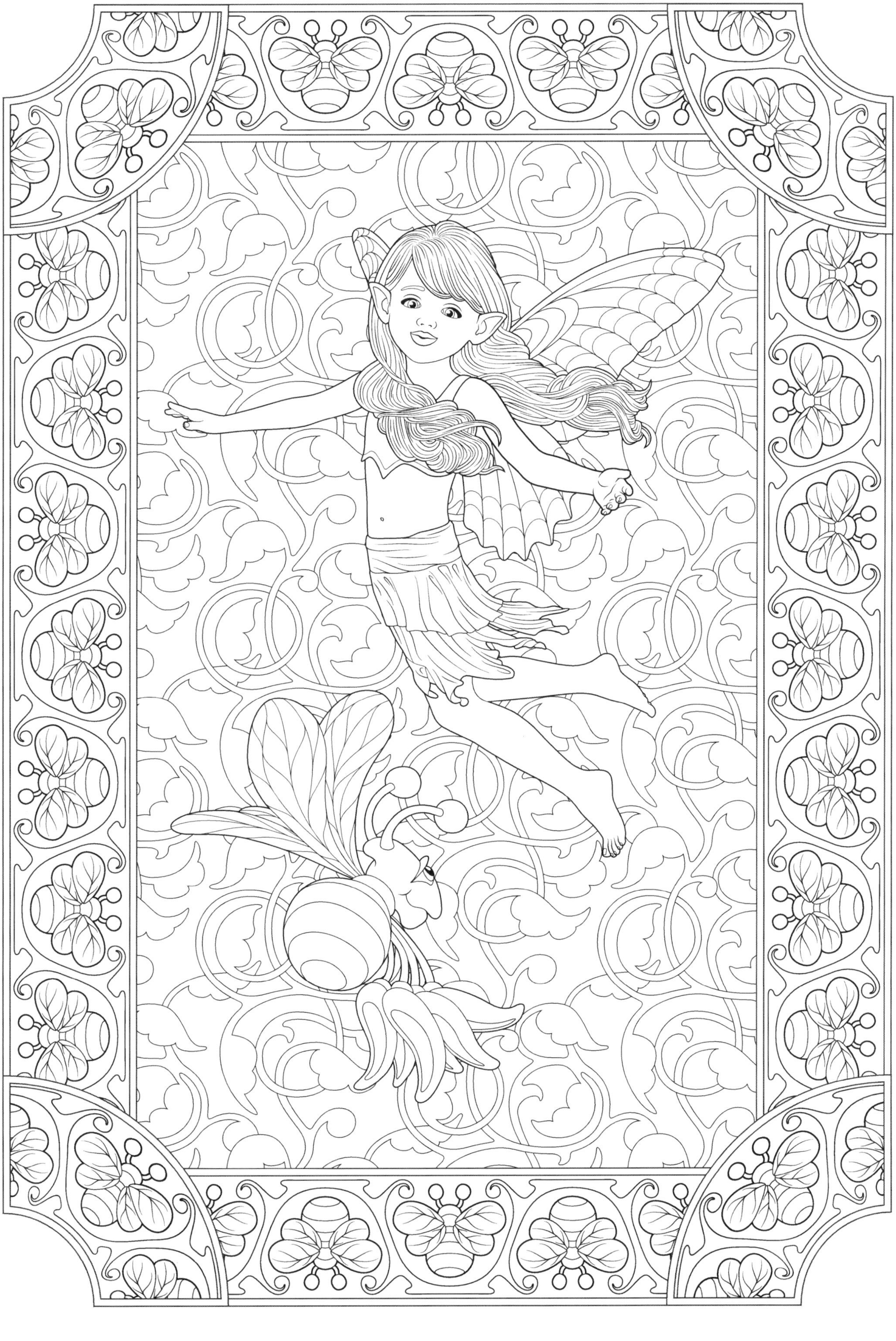

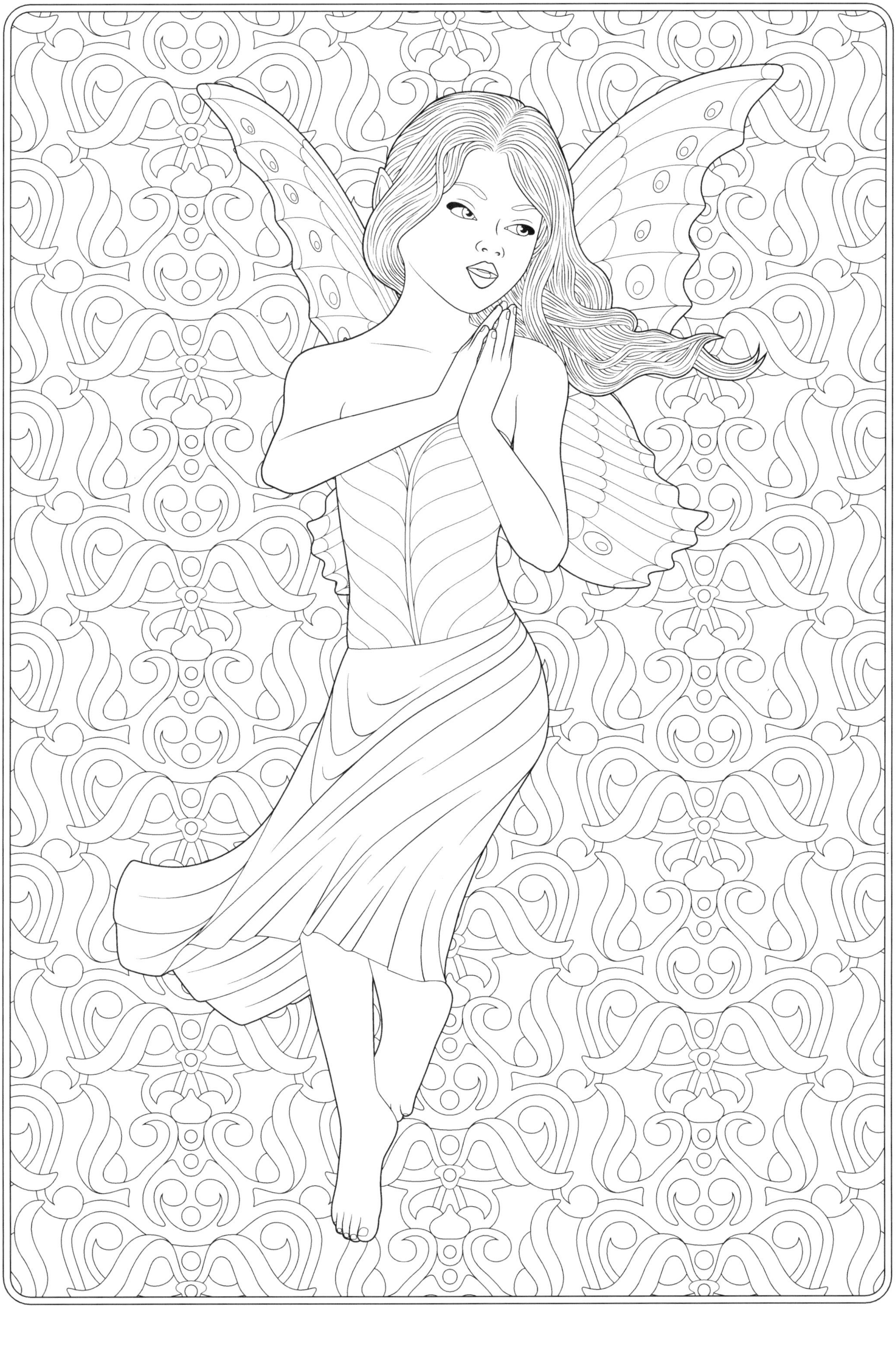

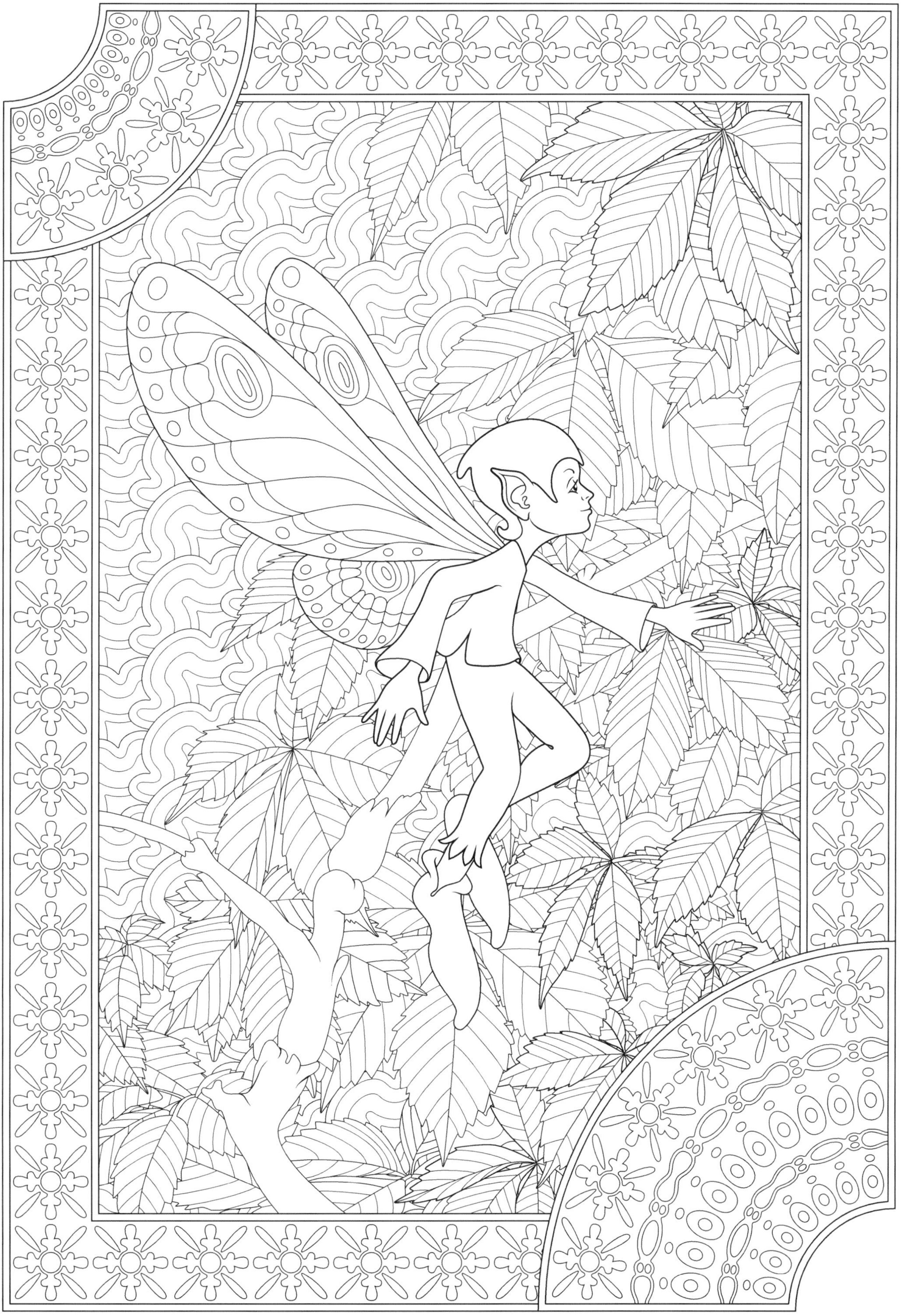

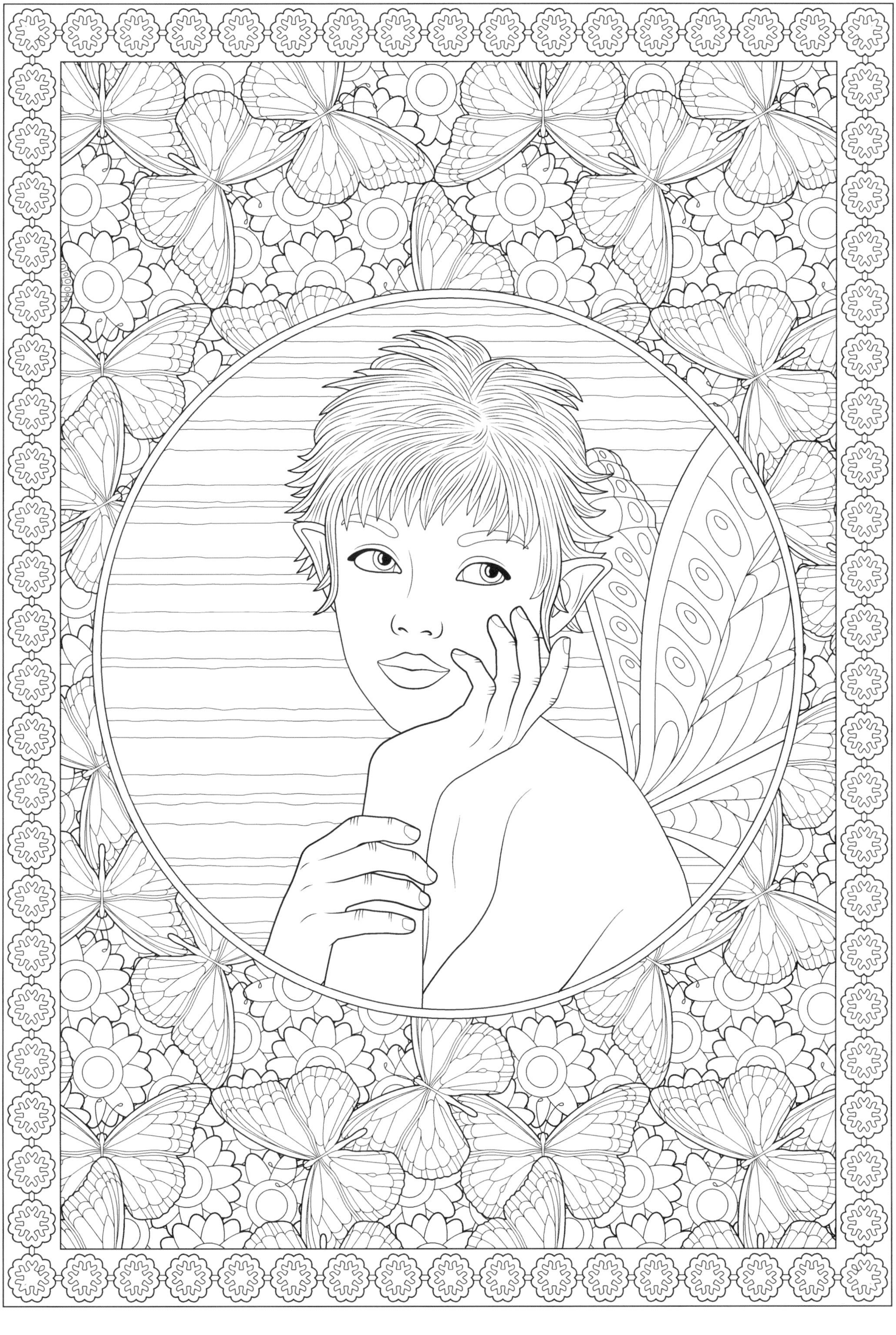

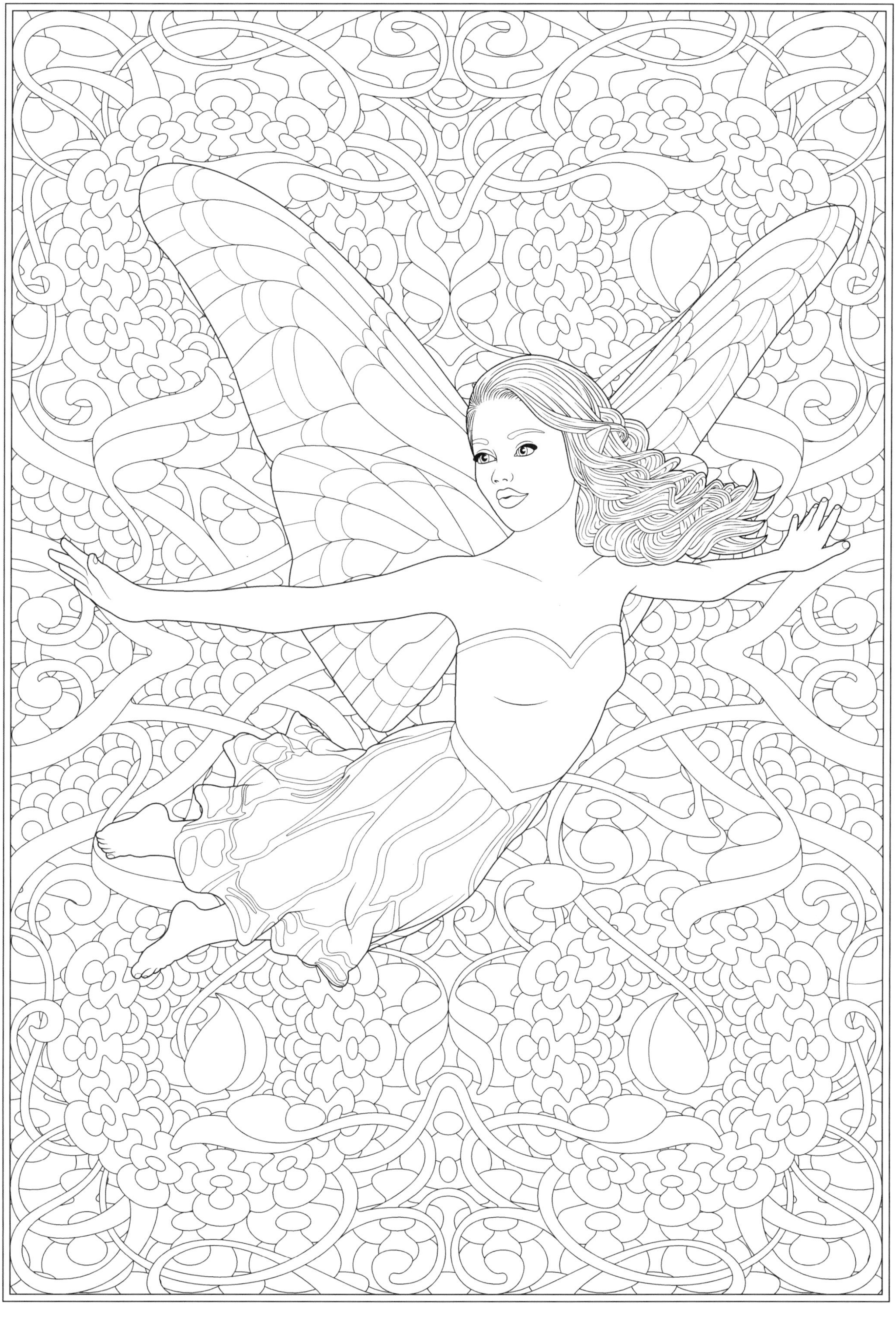

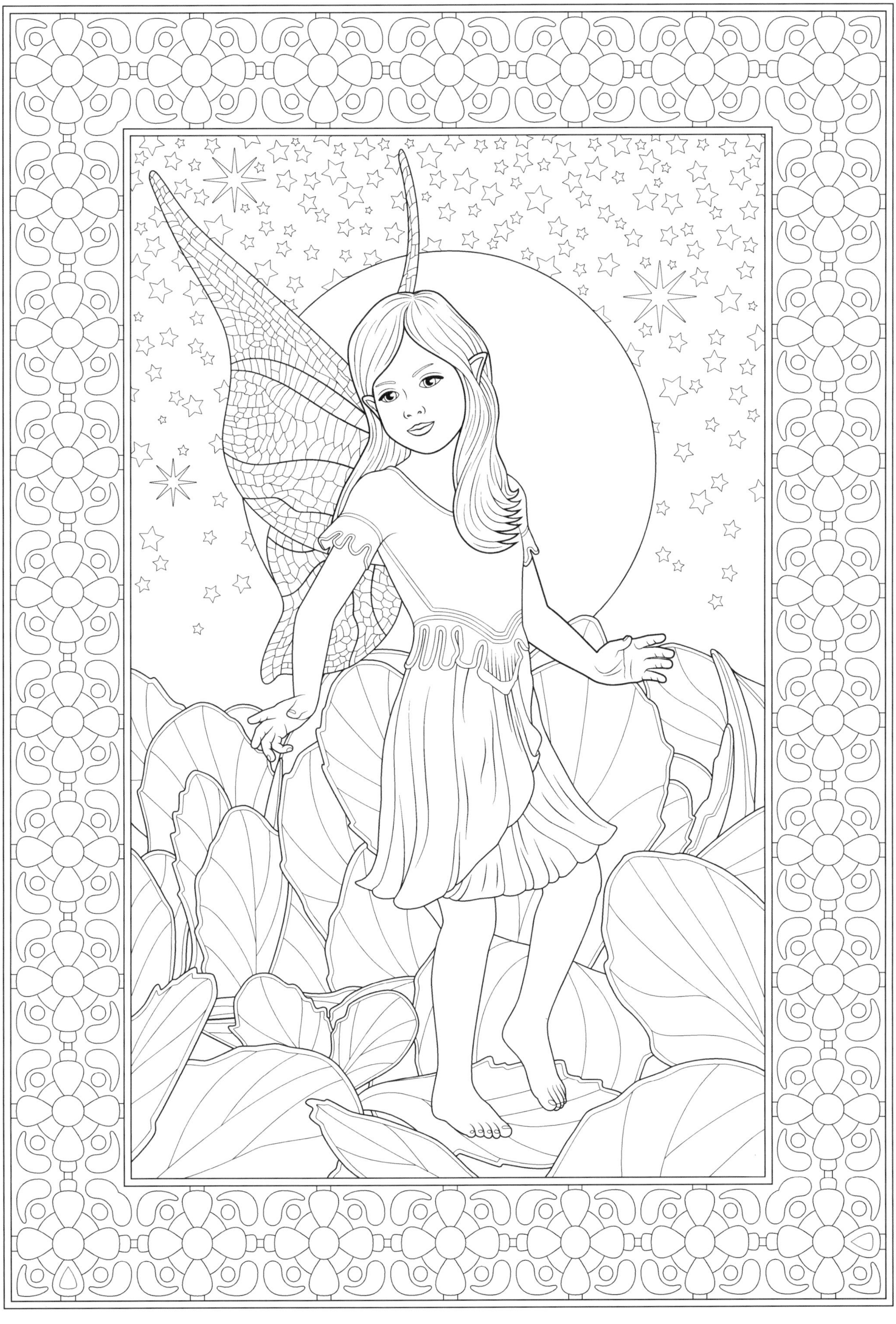

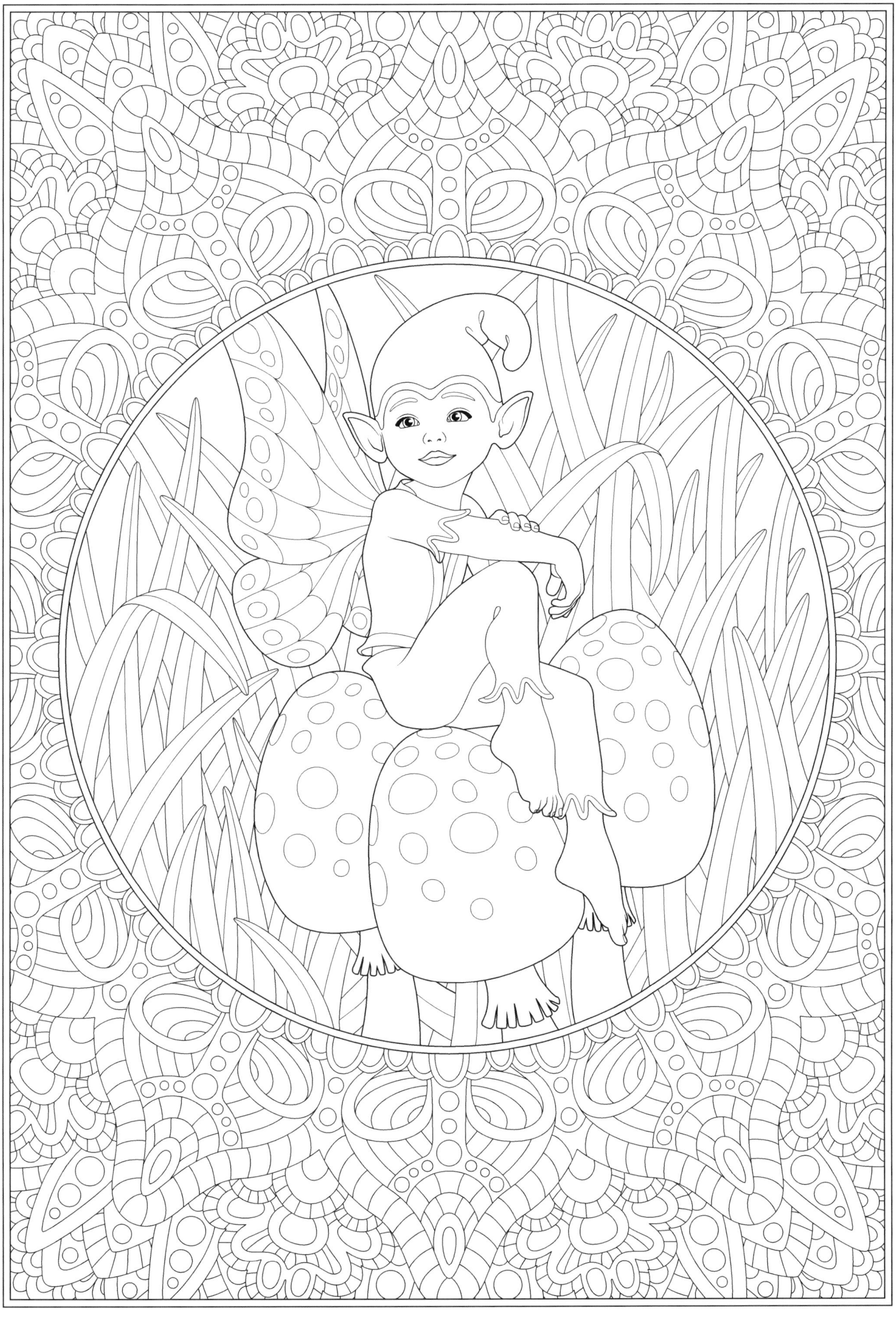

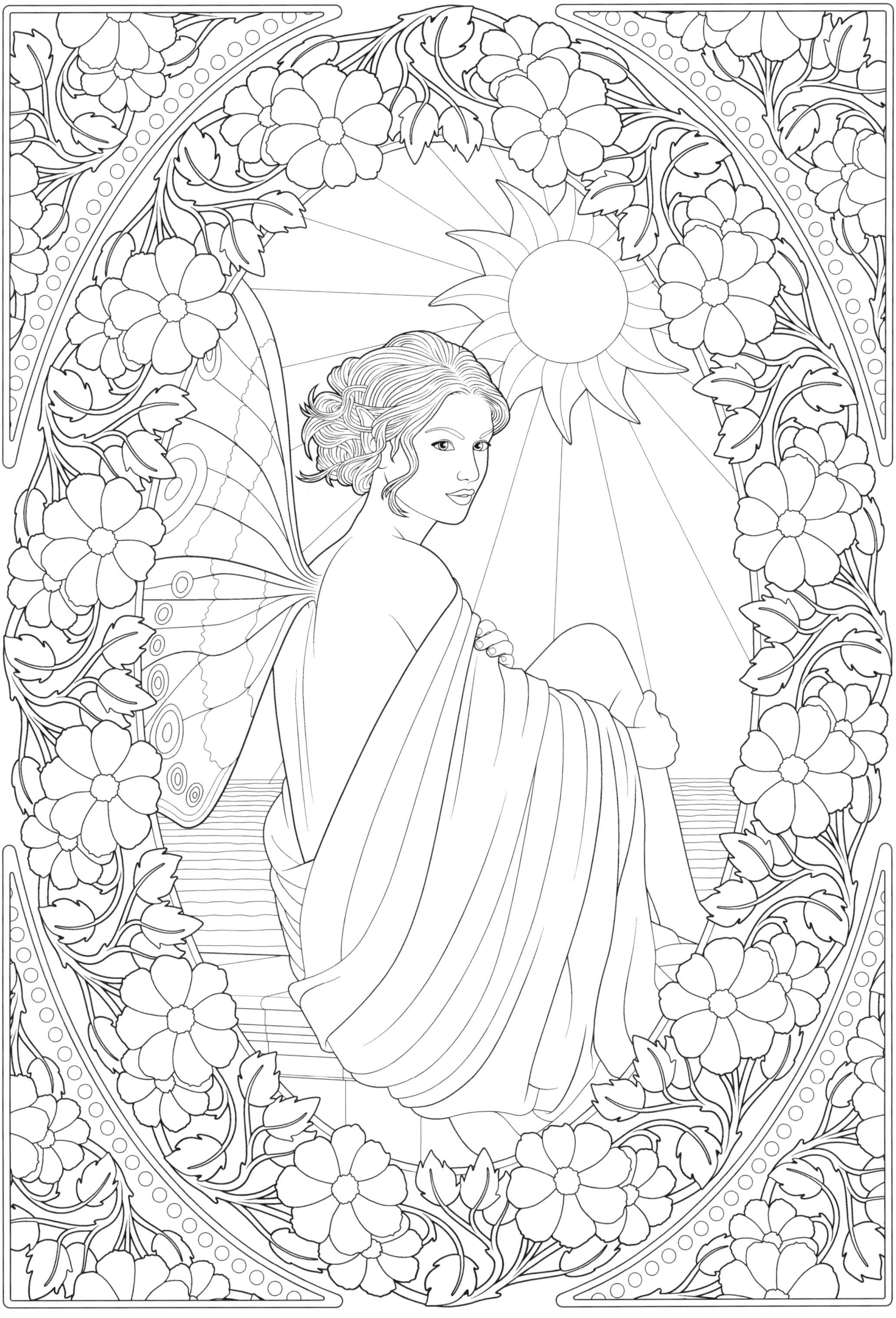

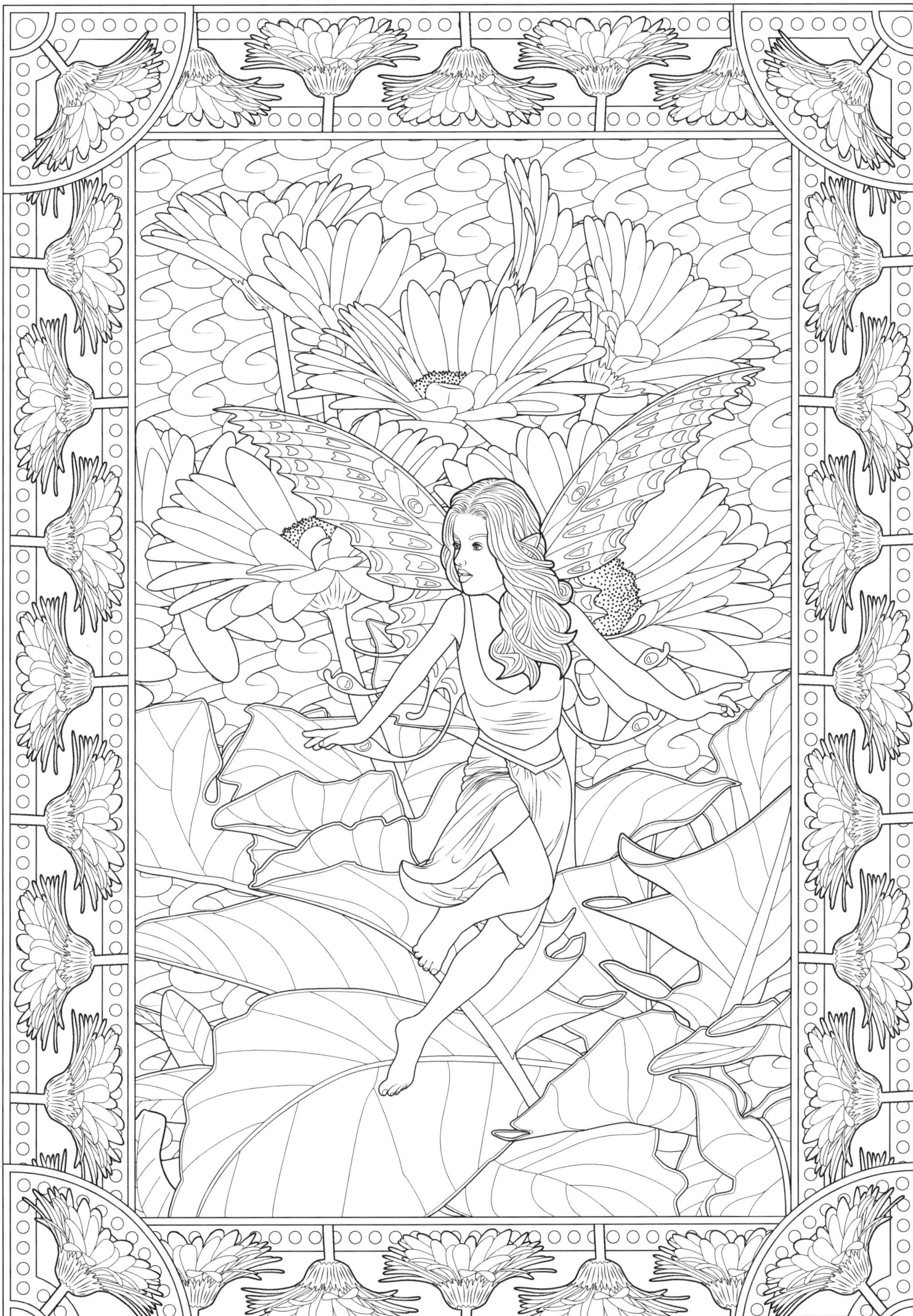

About the Artist

I'm an Australian born artist living in the USA.

Fairies, and all the gentler aspects of fantasy art, have been my passion since childhood.

I was educated in traditional fine art and spent decades painting with oils, acrylics, and egg tempera. These days, however, I paint and draw on a computer using all my previously hard-won traditional painting skills. Yep, such creative reinventions are indeed possible.

You can find more of my art here: **StephenJohnSmith.com**

Please Post a Review

If you've enjoyed this coloring book, please leave an honest review on *Amazon.* Reviews go a long way to increasing a book's visability in the *Amazon* store. Thank you.

And if you find yourself stumped about what to include in such a review, you might use the following questions as a starting point.

- What did you like most about the book?
- What about the book surprised you?
- Did the book cover the content as described?
- Do you think you got your money's worth?
- How does it compare to other books in this category? And please cite any book you'd compare this one to.

Don't forget you can also include photos of your finished colored art in the review!

Thanks again, and happy coloring!

Made in United States
Orlando, FL
21 September 2023